AUTHOR.

Be Welcome.

Greetings to all readers present here in this reading.

My name is Washington Luiz de Figueiredo Junior. I have a degree in computer science with multiple specializations on it, especially in the area of software development, automation, artificial intelligence, as well as mobile application development with extensive experience in UX - user experience and UI - user interface.

My experience in technology field, with over 20 years, as well as my personal experience as user and buyer, made me raise questions about multiple mistakes made by users or buyers, due to their lack of knowledge over the years. For these and other reasons, I´ve decided to gather all my knowledge here, in just a simple and a complete guidebook, to help guide these people in financial education in how to buy.

I am graduated from universities such as: UCB - Catholic University of Brasilia and UNIEURO. I´ve done courses and certifications from certified companies such as: Microsof, Sun, Novel, Cisco, among others. For the past 12 years I have only worked with mobile development from companies such as Apple, Google, Amazon and many others that only aimed at developing apps in order to gain more insight into new interface engines and to improve the mobile experience with users in their respective online markets.

SUMMARY.

Index

AUTHOR.
BE WELCOME..1

SUMMARY.
INDEX..2

INTRODUCTION.
HOW TO BUY WITH A FINANCIAL EDUCATION KNOWLEDGE........................3

MODULE 1 - BE PREPARED.
NO HELP AT THE RIGHT TIME..4
ALWAYS MAKE A LIST OF ALL PRODUCTS...5
QUANTITY OF PRODUCTS TO BE PURCHASED..6
SHOPS AND SITES WHERE YOUR PRODUCTS ARE SOLD................................7
AGILITY AND EFFICIENCY IN SEARCHING AND SHOPPING.............................8

MODULE 2 - PHYSICAL STORES.
HOURS AND ITINERARIES...9
CHEAPER PARTS IN THE SHOWCASE..10
OPENBOX PRODUCTS...11
TALK AND MAKE FRIENDSHIP WITH THE SELLERS.....................................12
ALWAYS CARRY YOUR MOBILE DEVICE TO ANSWER YOUR QUESTIONS.....13
ADVANTAGE TO GET THE PRODUCT NOW..14

MODULE 3 - ONLINE SHOPPING.
MAKE A LIST OF ADDRESSES..15
ONLINE SHOPPING CART..16
LIMITED QUANTITY..17
PRICE AND COUPONS...18
PRICE COMPARISON TOOLS FOR BROWSERS...19
SPECIALIZED SEARCHING WEBSITES..20
RESERVING PRODUCTS FOR DESIRED PRICE..21
FRAUD DETECTION AND FAKE SITES..22
SLOW PAGES WHEN THE TIME COMES...23

MODULE 4 - BUY FAST AND EFFICIENTLY.
DON´T BE UNDECIDED..24
HOW TO PREDICT THE FUTURE OF PRICES...25
IF TIME DOESN'T STOP THEN USE A TIMER...26
EVALUATE YOUR PURCHASES IN THE FUTURE AND BE HAPPY....................27
ABOUT..28

INTRODUCTION.

How to buy with a financial education knowledge.

Spending less and saving doesn't hurt anyone. It can be observed that over the past years most consumers do not know how to interact with current technology to assist them in their daily shopping. The lack of technology knowledge or simply the lack of behavioral direction makes today's consumers easy victims of the voracity of a globalizing markets with their technology advancements.

Financial education should be a basic discipline in today's high school. As the influence of knowledge in finance can directly affect the daily expenses of a person who often depends on little capital to live.

For these and others this reading will be devoted to passing on the maximum knowledge content I´ve learned and observed over the past years about how you, the consumer, can and should behave before and after you make your purchases, whether buying online or physical.

Anyone can become a shopping MASTER at any time. And every consumer can always pay less on any product.

Currently in our digital marketplace there is a range of tools and gadgets to assist consumers from different standards in the practice of their daily shopping and not just during the Black Friday season, which will be covered here.

This reading will do its utmost to transform the vision of those who want to become independent specialized buyers in online shopping and physical stores, making possible reasonable capital savings at a Black Friday season or at any purchase every day.

MODULE 1 – BE PREPARED

No help at the right time.

Many consumers have come across the kind of situation where most lack the knowledge to make a purchase or simply depend on someone else who was not available at the time.

Even today, questions about how to make a simple online purchase or how to securely pay using a credit card, and even about finding a good store to buy a specific product, are the most common doubts in inexperienced consumers.

If your buyer profile is qualified as an inexperienced person, don't worry! Since the content proposed in this reading is to make you a more experienced consumer in the area of shopping and at the same time to further enrich the knowledge of those who already have a certain wisdom.

In our lives everything is reflected in our behavior and discipline. And when it comes to buying, this too could not be different. But how to prepare for a globalized and voracious market that can't stop breathing? It is with this thought that financial education becomes the best input for knowledge and answers to questions.

Always make a list of all products.

Here we will start practicing a basic exercise that we will do before making any kind of purchase. The consumer side basis from a healthy financial behavior comes from the initial creation of a simple shopping list for everything we want to spend our money on. In the Black Friday week we will often have no time to keep up with all the offers. This is when we will have in hand or on a device a paper or a text file containing all the products we are interested in purchasing.

Make a list of all the products you are interested in and put a minimum price and an acceptable maximum price in your budget. Always research prices throughout the year until the last week before the Black Friday day. Classic example:

- SHARP 4K TV 65 INCHES -------------------------- from $698,00 to $298,00.
- SAMSUNG REFRIGERATOR 25.5 CU ------------ from $2199,97 to $999,97.

In case the product has not been released yet, still put it on your list, as this will also be your desired list of products to buy in the future:

- FRIGIDAIRE DISHWASHER ----------------------------- from $429,99 to $299,97.
- 5-BURNERS SAMSUNG STOVE ------------------------ from $1099,97 to $599,97.
- PS4 GAME GTA6 (ASSUMED 03/01/2022) --------- from $59,99 to $45,99.

Do not forget any products and also put the gifts you will buy for Christmas.

Black Friday is not a "Black Fraud" and your shopping will be cheaper.

Quantity of products to be purchased.

At the time of a Black Friday week, be aware that the maximum number of products sold will be limited per buyer.

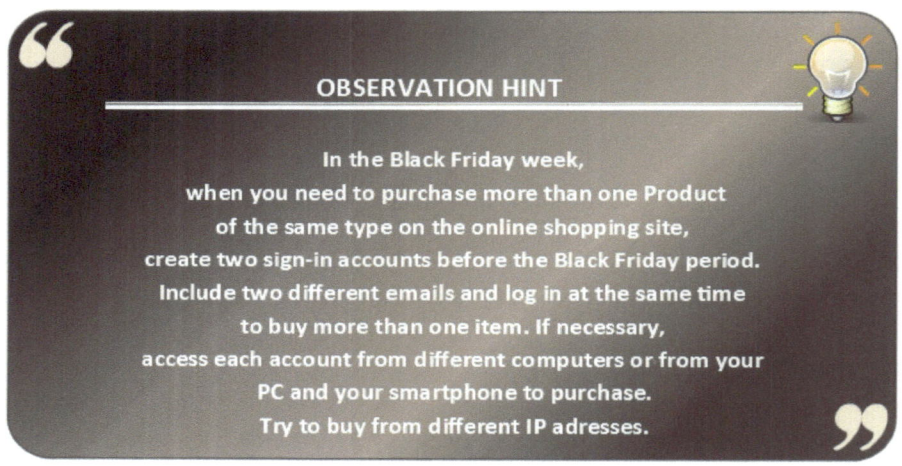

OBSERVATION HINT

In the Black Friday week, when you need to purchase more than one Product of the same type on the online shopping site, create two sign-in accounts before the Black Friday period. Include two different emails and log in at the same time to buy more than one item. If necessary, access each account from different computers or from your PC and your smartphone to purchase. Try to buy from different IP adresses.

Remember that the shipping amount will also be counted on each product of the same type purchased from different email accounts.

Do not exceed the amount of the same item to be purchased as it may also affect the value of shipping to the same address.

Respect other buyers and don't buy too much to resell. Remember that all consumers have the same right to buy and that everyone will get their chance on Black Friday. Buying too much can cause retailers to adjust the prices of these products making them more expensive.

Shops and sites where your products are sold.

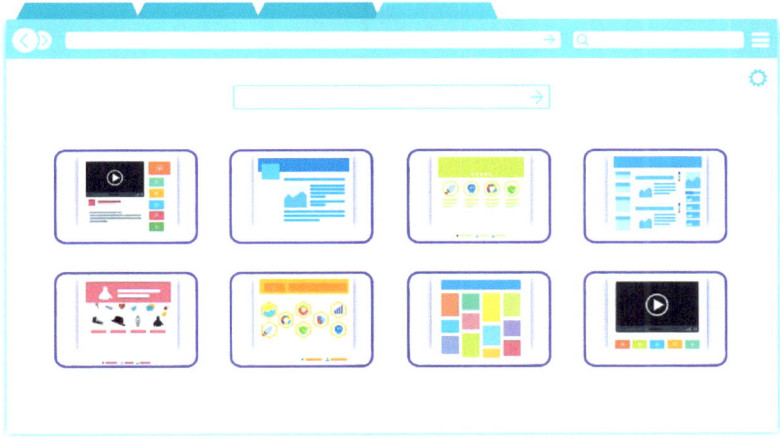

To properly prepare for an event like the Black Friday week review and compare product prices daily. Create a custom bookmark in your web browser of your choice and add sites with the following categories:

- Online search engines like Google.
- Product search sites like Slickdeals.
- Coupon sites to apply when paying to lower prices.
- Discussion forum links that promote products on Black Friday.
- Price comparators to evaluate promotions.

Save this bookmark and send a saved copy to a trusted email. This bookmark will be the most used item in your online shopping and also in pricing when you are in a physical store with your mobile device.

In the case of purchases at physical stores, make a note of the updated addresses and telephone numbers in your calendar, as well as their opening time. Make a prior visit and talk to some sellers. The famous saying "Whoever has a mouth goes to Rome" applies perfectly here. With charisma and education you can discover the days of in-store promotions and befriend sellers who can even book orders in advance.

Agility and efficiency in searching and shopping.

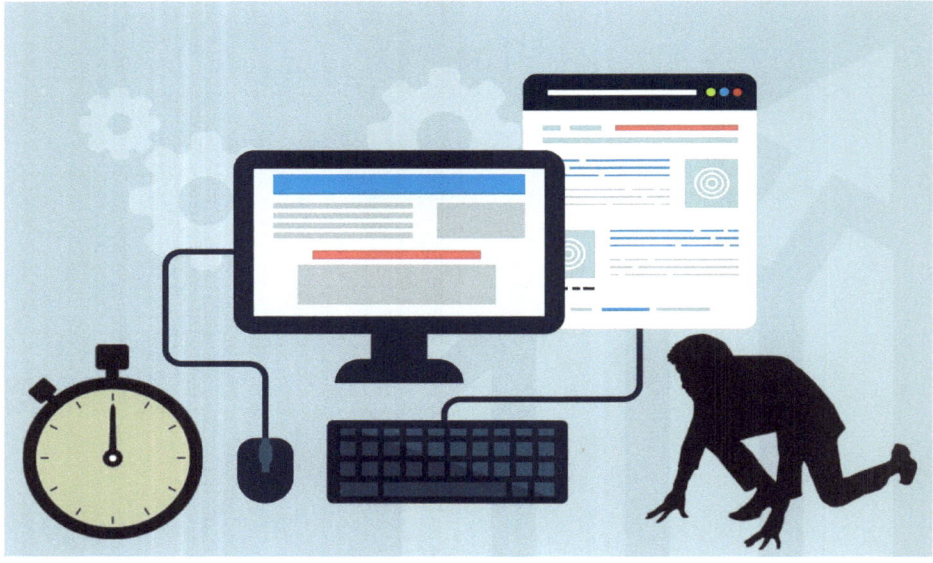

Black Friday week is short and it goes by very fast.

Agility in action must be prepared in advance. It´s no use for the buyer to have only the money in hands, you must be prepared to make decisions and to search quickly and efficiently.

In the short week of promotions, be prepared to go out and take your mobile device when buying at physical stores so you won´t miss any online promotions.

Be connected in discussion forums, as consumers there will post promotion messages occurring in real time at certain physical stores and online selling sites.

Access your bookmarks even away from home with your mobile device and stay tuned for promotions within physical stores.

The conclusion of this first module literally boils down to: be prepared or prepare initially and don't underestimate promotions. The Black Friday never stops to wait.

MODULE 2 - PHYSICAL STORES.

Hours and itineraries.

Once you have noted all the store addresses and times on your calendar, set aside time on Black Friday week that always begins one week before the official day on November 29th. The largest stores will be preparing for the official day on 29th at 18:00 o'clock, but your objective here will be to monitor all your desired products since the previous week for any price changes in products. Remember that many retailers will be offering promotions even before November 29th. The same will be done the weeks after the Black Friday day where several shopkeepers will be offering clearance prices of their inventory left over in their stores.

Several products on your list will surely be in these promotions. Review each one and track the change in prices.

Talk to sellers for important tips on promotions and clearance sales after the Black Friday. Dialogue and charisma will be your greatest weapon here. You may also be able to carry pamphlets from other stores and ask sellers if they can further cover their offers.

Cheaper parts in the showcase.

Yes my dear reader, here is one of the most important tips when buying expensive electronics or home appliances products at physical stores. If you really want to pay even cheaper than deals on a Black Friday ask for the last showcase product.

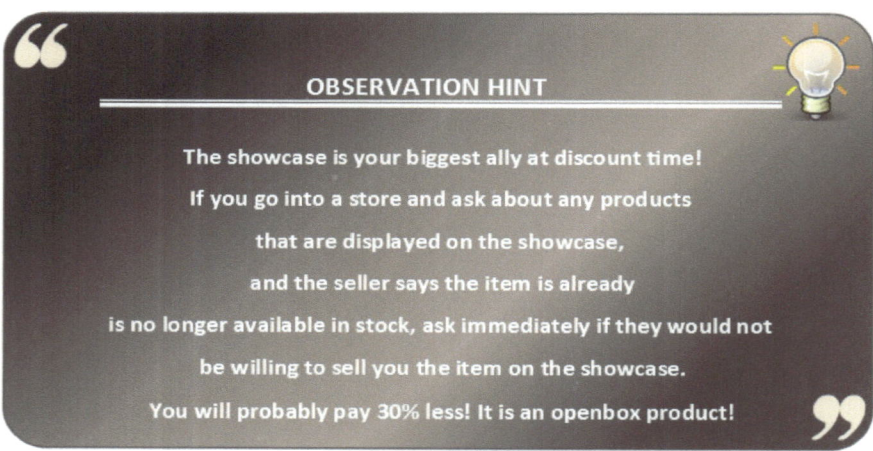

OBSERVATION HINT

The showcase is your biggest ally at discount time! If you go into a store and ask about any products that are displayed on the showcase, and the seller says the item is already is no longer available in stock, ask immediately if they would not be willing to sell you the item on the showcase. You will probably pay 30% less! It is an openbox product!

Products or showcased items, which usually have no box, but comes with the manual and all items that were inside their box. In addition to the value of the Black Friday promotion week, this showcased item is likely to have its value reduced even further by its openbox condition. There are people who have already purchased complete showcase parts and kits and have paid up less than 40% of their original value. Use this tip and be a happy buyer.

Openbox products.

Here is one of the golden egg chickens of the Black Friday week.

OpenBox products or simply repackaged products. These are items that were opened inside stores, as well as showcase merchandise, but also bought and returned by consumers who did not appreciate the product. The reasons may be varied, but the main one is a slight defect such as a scratch, a dent or simply these products did not fit the expectations of their buyers not fitting in their homes.

The OpenBox merchandise can be located both within regular stores and at stores specializing in the sale of these products. There are currently several stores specializing only in OpenBox merchandise resale. Ask physical store sellers to which companies they forward their returned OpenBox items and, if possible, get their address. Or do a Google search and find these stores in your area.

The resale values can be reduced up to 70 percent off during promotion seasons. Many of these OpenBox products may have slight defects as mentioned earlier. But take into consideration the fact that they will be working perfectly and will still have guarantees on your purchase. This guarantee will also accompany the factory warranty of the product.

Most OpenBox products have a data list, informing you of the product return issue. So don't worry about buying an OpenBox merchandise, as you will also be protected by the consumer code.

Talk and make friendship with the sellers.

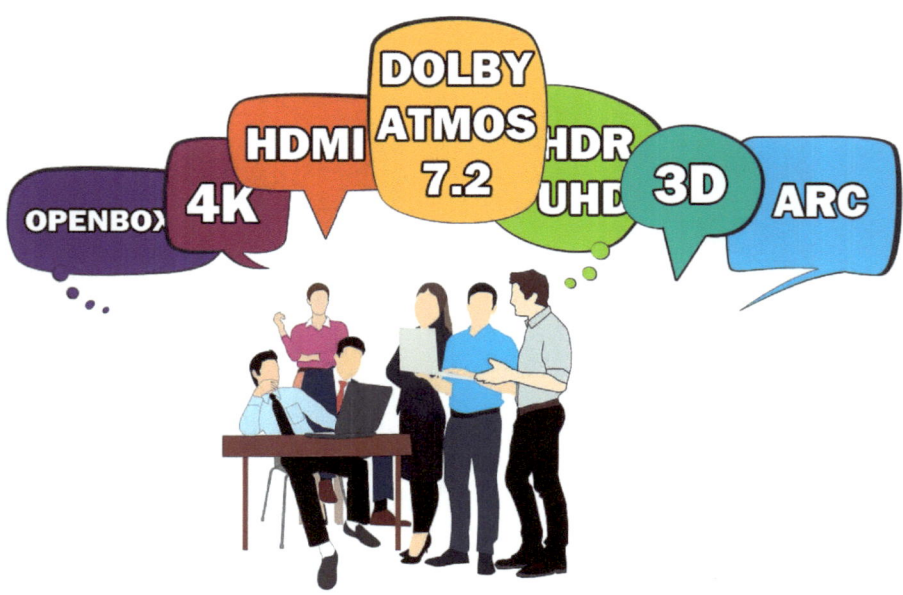

Technology is present every day in our lives. Therefore there is nothing fairer than the search for knowledge and the understanding of it.

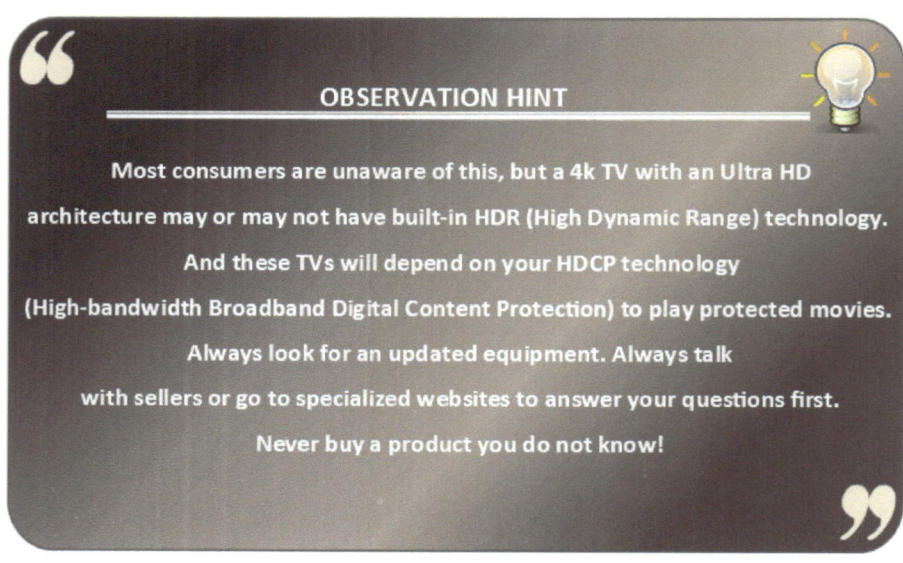

> **OBSERVATION HINT**
>
> Most consumers are unaware of this, but a 4k TV with an Ultra HD architecture may or may not have built-in HDR (High Dynamic Range) technology. And these TVs will depend on your HDCP technology (High-bandwidth Broadband Digital Content Protection) to play protected movies. Always look for an updated equipment. Always talk with sellers or go to specialized websites to answer your questions first.
> Never buy a product you do not know!

Conversation and dialogue can be the key to solving daily problems. Make the most of your conversation with professionals and technicians who are present in physical stores and online forums to answer your questions and learn more about technology.

Always carry your mobile device to answer your questions.

When shopping at physical stores never forget to bring your best friend, your mobile device. Always be on the lookout for information between products and for information given by vendors who are unsure of their specification. Buying non-Bivolt equipment, for example, and plugging it in can make your investment burn.

Searching engines such as Google, Yahoo, or product review sites like CNET, or YouTube itself can help a lot outside home. For more accurate questions about a product, visit YouTube and watch full product reviews. If even the seller has questions about a product forward the correct information to him as well.

Always try to research your products on technology forums or websites that constantly evaluate these goods. The promotion may be tempting at the moment, but if you are unsure of the characteristics from a particular product, do not buy it. The regret will be greater if you spend your money without having an use for it. If you are thinking of buying to resell, do a complete research on prices and see if it will be worth it. Never buy a pig in a poke.

Always use your calculator to evaluate the spot price and the parceled price from products. Do not trust 100 percent in the calculation passed on by the sellers, because making mistakes is part of the human being. Also calculate the tax of your region. Write down the values from products already purchased, in your calendar, and always check how much has already been spent on your budget. Don't underestimate the excitement of a Black Friday thrill, as you will end up spending more than you should.

Advantage to get the product now.

Here's the biggest reason why you leave the comfort of your home to shop for the Black Friday´s week at a physical store. you are Guaranteed to receive your merchandise at the time of purchase. All of course will depend on stock availability.

Shopping at online stores can be wonderful, but waiting for up to a whole week can be stressful when making a final evaluation of your purchase.

Be aware that inside stores you will be competing for a stock burn, announced by a megaphone. At this time, do not despair and do not run like a crazy person. First check the location, within the store, of this promotion's department, and go as soon as possible to check for this stock burn. Many people, at these times, run wildly over everything and even destroying other products to find out, in the end, that they have no interest in taking this promotion. Keep calm and remember that any damage caused should be compensated for your actions.

Clearance sale promotions, inside stores, can also be reported by phone. Interested friends and family can be notified, and if there is an interest, you can pick up other duplicate items from the same promotion yourself and expect your acquaintances to come at the store. Or simply to pay and repost the products later. In this case remember that it will depend on the maximum quantity you will be allowed to buy.

Have fun shopping at physical stores and don't forget to bring your mobile device to search.

MODULE 3 - ONLINE SHOPPING.

Make a list of addresses.

From the week before Black Friday 29th to the week after, set aside a few hours and get ready for a real online battle. Open those addresses previously listed in your already saved bookmarks and get ready to work.

Access your previously listed product file to quickly evaluate the top products that will necessarily be required for your purchases. Make a quick priority evaluation and mark the first items to look for. Go to a search page like Google and type words like your product name with synonyms or adjectives like: promotion, discount, stock burn, coupon, promobug, black friday, shops, cheap, clearance sales, low price or any other information you are looking for about the product on sale.

Enter search pages and forums such as:

- The Pepper Network world page available every day:
- https://www.pepper.com/.
- Slickdeals forum for promotions and sales coupons: https://slickdeals.net/forums/.
- Black Friday's own promotion site with Ad Scans too:
- https://blackfriday.com/.

If you need, make your registration and ask about any questions.

Online shopping cart.

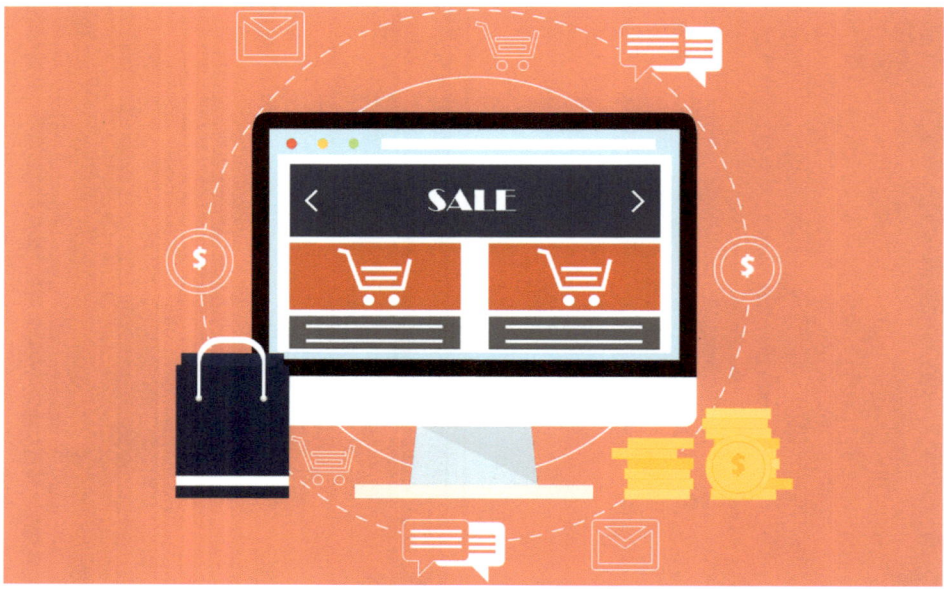

Hesitation when buying a product at the height of the offers is most common in Black Friday´s week. Promotions do not stop popping up and you will constantly wonder whether or not that particular item may fall even further in price.

When a very good promotion comes along and you still have questions. Make use of your best partner when shopping online, the shopping cart.

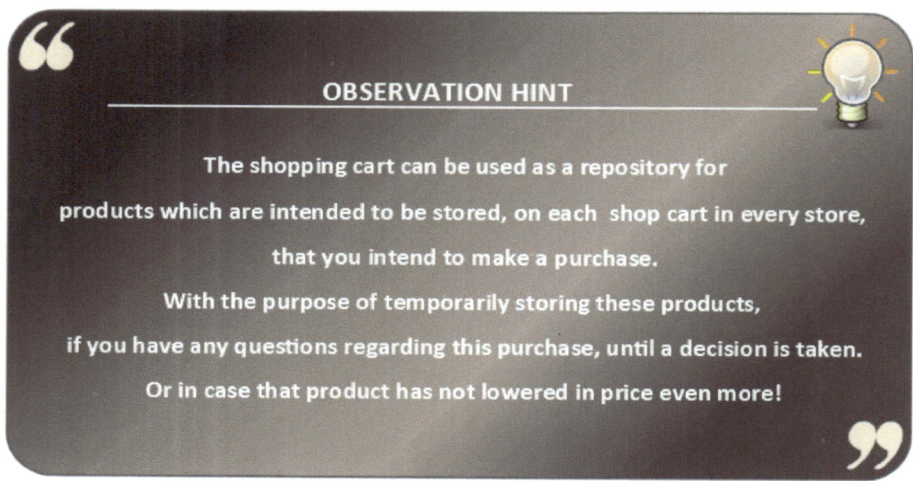

OBSERVATION HINT

The shopping cart can be used as a repository for products which are intended to be stored, on each shop cart in every store, that you intend to make a purchase.
With the purpose of temporarily storing these products, if you have any questions regarding this purchase, until a decision is taken.
Or in case that product has not lowered in price even more!

Always check the quantity allowed on each shopping site and be sure to calculate the total shipping values for each product inside the shopping cart adding your taxes.

Limited quantity.

The foundation of an adequate financial education comes from good manners. And it would not be correct to say that a person can buy as much as he wants when he wants to. Remember that each individual is part of a large and organized society and everyone has the same rights and duties. Respect other consumers at the time of purchase, and place only the items you really want to buy on your cart. Remove useless items from shopping carts in online stores. The Black Friday only happens once a year so if all consumers buy correctly everyone will benefit.

When removing unnecessary items, from the shopping cart, make a quick evaluation or talk to friends and family, in advance, as they may be interested in those products.

Be sure to check the possibility of using coupons in every online store where your products are being hosted in the shopping carts.

Don't remove products that you still have questions about buying at once. The Black Friday Week promotions should not be underestimated and these prices may never reach again the same discount standard.

Remember the well-known popular saying "the habit makes the monk" so practice it daily in your online shopping and behave well towards other consumers because "What goes around, comes around" and you are also inside this community of consumers.

Price and coupons.

Do you know what a coupon is?

A coupon is an object that features a discount promotion code for some product, product type, or even for a specific store. The product prices in Black Friday's week may fall by up to 30 percent or less. But you can bring that price down even further by applying a coupon when you make your purchase at Checkout (payment) or within the shopping cart. A coupon can be divided between:

- Directional Coupon - directs you to the discount page or products.
- Code Coupon - Issues a code to be applied to the shopping cart.
- Card Coupons - Sign up for the store loyalty card for discounts and special coupons. These may even be physical coupons or virtual credits.

There are even coupons to give free shipping exclusively for heavier products. Several coupon sites are available online, but some famous pages for coupon tracking today are:

- Amazon Coupons - https://amazon.com/coupons
- Living Social - https://www.livingsocial.com/
- Groupon - https://www.groupon.com
- Swagbucks - https://www.swagbucks.com
- Slickdeals - https://slickdeals.net/
- Rakuten - https://www.rakuten.com

When you search for a specific coupon, type in Google the store name followed by the word coupon or the product name followed by the word coupon. There are online stores that even allow you to use more than one coupon on their websites. Make the most of these coupons even outside the Black Friday season. You may be amazed at the final value of your purchases.

Price comparison tools for browsers.

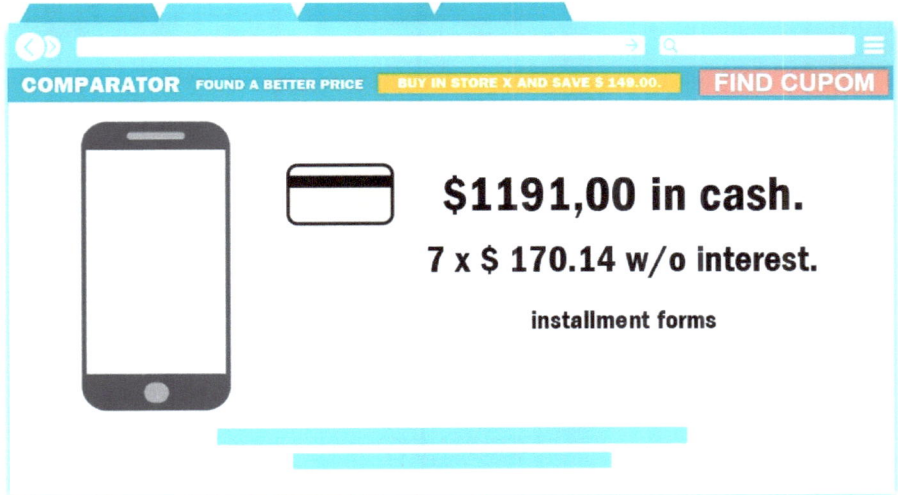

Price comparators are browser extensions that serve to:

- Compare prices from onl ine stores and pass to users the l owest prices.
- To search for coupons automatically for the websites of the stores that you visit.
- Find and apply a coupon automatically when paying for a product in the cart.

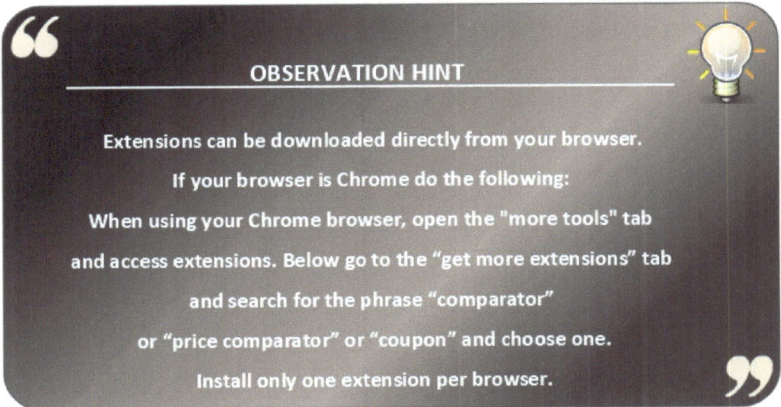

If an installed comparator is used, when buying a product in one store, the program will automatically inform you the price of that product in other stores and present the lowest value. When you pay at Checkout and click on the enter coupon tab, the program will search for the best coupon available for that store and apply it. Here I will not list the programs, because the list would be too long. Read the user's review and install only the best one.

Specialized searching websites.

In Black Friday periods a variety of websites that post updated promotions will be available to all consumers. These specialized search engines provide a list of products with the best up-to-date discounts and a list of coupons for each specific store for each of these items.

Some specialized websites even have a registration for desired products that will be on your shopping list. If a reserved product on your wishing list gets a promotion, the site will automatically send an email for the user to be informed.

Some websites specialized in promotions with a wish list:

- https://bestblackfriday.com/
- https://www.walmart.com/
- https://www.target.com
- https://www.amazon.com/
- https://www.bestbuy.com/
- https://www.samsclub.com/

Keep in mind that most of these sites will not be available only at the Black Friday week, but all year long. Also you can check their mobile Apps for special offers too. So use their services whenever you want to purchase some merchandise online. Enjoy the convenience of the wishlist service and create your desired list. And when your product features a promotion apply a coupon when you pay and be happy saving.

Reserving products for desired price.

The vast majority of people are unaware of this, but many promotion sites and even discussion forums have a database that can book the product you want to buy and even register it for a specific price.

How many online shoppers would not like to receive a dream promotion directly on their email or in their social networks? These buyers simply do not know the functionality of the services offered on specialized sales pages and especially during the Black Friday week.

Try to use the product registration service on promotion sites to even register the maximum and minimum price range you are looking for for certain products.

Often with your daily chores, you will not be available to access websites and forums constantly. In the Black Friday period the same will happen, causing a specific promotion to be lost. This is when a product registration on specialized websites will be a great ally. When registering a product, be sure to check the name or code of the item and evaluate the price range you want to pay. Don´t forget to add the shipping value, the product fees and if you are on Black Friday week never underestimate the minimum discount that you can get. Remember that retailers can spread PromoBugs online to attract consumers and often these PromoBugs can temporarily lower prices by up to 70% the value of the products.

Fraud detection and fake sites.

Do you know what the term phishing means?
The phishing is a dishonest way that cybercriminals use to trick you into revealing personal information, such as passwords, credit cards, social security numbers, and bank account numbers. They can make this by sending you fake emails or directing you to fake websites.

In the Black Friday period Phishing can be avoided with just a few basic rules of online behavior. When making a search or a purchase you have to:

- Verify the email address for these promotions.
- Evaluate the provenance of the website or online store.
- Evaluate the price of products.
- Evaluate the consumers responses.

Stores with new or unfamiliar names should be avoided as much as possible. Never make a purchase on a website or online store without knowing where they are coming from. Remember that hackers and cybercriminals can easily fool people online. The price may be tempting, but, if you have any doubt do not take a risk and go out buying any product without knowing it´s origin. Be wise and research a lot before you pay. Phishing's biggest function here is to get data from your credit card.

Evaluating on complaint sites or forums can be a good option to know about the provenance of websites and stores. The employer Identification Number (ENI) verification will also tell you a lot about those stores. The federal trade commission (FTC) page and complaint sites that may help identify fraud:

- The FTC page (protecting america's consumers) https://www.ftc.gov
- Consumer Affairs https://www.consumeraffairs.com
- Pissed Consumer https://www.pissedconsumer.com
- Complaint Board https://www.complaintsboard.com
- Hissing Kitty https://www.hissingkitty.com

Slow pages when the time comes.

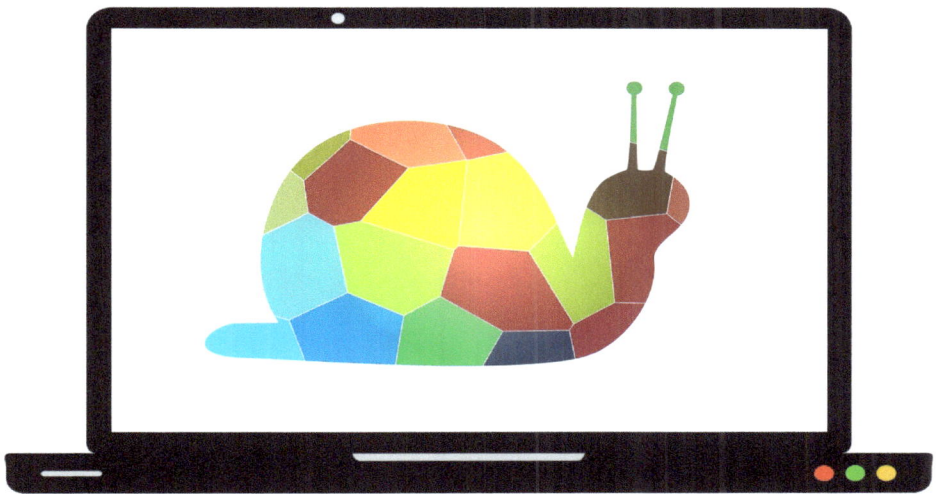

One of the biggest headaches in the Black Friday week is the slowness of pages due to the congestion of the online trafic. Pages and websites of major retailers may become extremely slow or even fall down losing their access.

To try to prevent your shopping from being hampered, keep calm and make use of the shopping cart features. Always try to allocate your products in the shopping carts. If you can complete your purchase remember that, even not using a coupon it will still result in a promotional purchase, because you are on the Black Friday week. Make a quick evaluation of the total amount to be paid and make your purchase if you wish. Remember the wise proverb "A bird in the hand is worth two in the bush" and don´t think twice.

Don´t forget that several people will be going through the same situation. The basic rule of a healthy financial behavior comes from common thinking:

- Be responsible when buying.
- Always print your receipt of purchase or payment.
- Stay within your minimum purchase limit (one unit per product).
- Be quick to access websites, if you can, and don't spend too much time with open pages.

If a purchase is unsuccessful or declined or returned by any store, do not worry and do not panic. Try your best to work around the situation even if you are angry. Contact the store and always show prints that were taken from your purchases or payments. Talk to the sellers and remember that making mistakes is a human act. And that slowness in the process can be avoided offline.

MODULE 4 - BUY FAST AND EFFICIENTLY.

Don´t be undecided.

Many consumers find the Black Friday period to be a scam some people even naming it as a Black Fraud event. With fallacies that buyers would pay half of the double the price for fake promotions. But that's not true! It's Black Friday´s week when you buy an expensive product for a cheaper price and often pay 30-70 percent less. Many shopkeepers to empty their unsold stocks in their stores will be willing to greatly reduce their values. So when shopping at Black Friday, don't think twice!

As an example, on the Black Friday of 2017, from my personal experience I´ve spent only $768.00 on products that after my final evaluation would have been spent around $2300.00. Many products were on sale and the vast majority of retailers were desperate to empty their stocks. An undecided act of buying something now will become in regret later and consequently lead you to spend more on products that were on sale but could not be well evaluated. Therefore always rate all your previous Black Friday purchases. You will agree that both the fallacies from others and your indecision about the event count only as a harmfull way in your quest for a better financial behavior to save on your shopping everyday.

How to predict the future of prices.

A characteristic of a consumer who is knowledgeable in the field of financial education is that he knows how to evaluate and predict the price value of the products.

You as a consumer should always:

- Have an organized list, register the amount of your monthly expenses and the amount spent in November with your Black Friday.
- Record the most expensive products you want to buy in the year and note their price changes each month.
- Evaluate and predict price change based on current market behavior.

The market forecasting is not a simple matter, but a critical estimation can be made based on price changes over the course of the year and with the changing from the market behavior. This market behavior can be influenced by several factors the main ones being linked to consumer´s demand, supply in certain products and the euphoria of the Black Friday´s week. Where shopkeepers get more optimistic about their sales even to clear their stranded inventory.

Therefore try your best to educate yourself financially to have a healthier consumer life. This "health" described here is nothing more than spending less and being able to evaluate your purchases not only on the Black Friday, but on your daily purchases.

If time doesn't stop then use a timer.

Online auction sites can be used to buy new or used products at low prices. These sites have a system similar to the physical auction where the highest bidder can take the item until it ends.

Few know a technique widely used by professional online auction buyers. The technique of using a stopwatch.

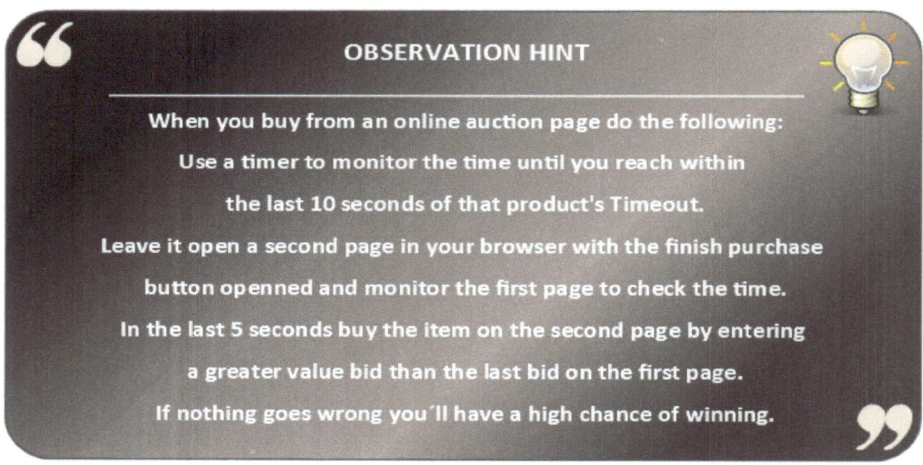

OBSERVATION HINT

When you buy from an online auction page do the following:
Use a timer to monitor the time until you reach within the last 10 seconds of that product's Timeout.
Leave it open a second page in your browser with the finish purchase button openned and monitor the first page to check the time.
In the last 5 seconds buy the item on the second page by entering a greater value bid than the last bid on the first page.
If nothing goes wrong you´ll have a high chance of winning.

This technique has been used several times and tested by personal experience. It is a valid technique and is sure to make it easier for you to win at an online auction. To give you an idea, even some players using this tip at the Blizzard company´s PC game Diablo 3 in it´s real money auction house have managed to get rich just by trading within the game. Therefore, every online auction is subject to a facilitation by the use of just one simple timer.

Evaluate your purchases in the future and be happy.

With so many devices and techniques quoted and the modeling of proper financial behavior, exemplified here in this reading, any individual will be able to better manage their purchases and consequently spend less when buying.

Always remember to:

- Keep your spending notes up-to-date by always registering your products and average price before purchasing any products. The basic idea is to make a list for everything you buy or to compare.
- Check and evaluate, in advance, the best physical store or online where this particular product is located. Always keep updated addresses and itineraries.
- Search for the best deals, coupons, OpenBox stores or any opportunity to get your product cheap and with guarantee.
- Always be prepared quickly for decision making and never regret your purchases. Be agile and effective when it comes to buying.
- To know how to evaluate your purchases and promotions on Black Friday or in your daily purchases.

This is a basic summary of the modules described here in this EBook for any user to exercise in their daily shopping and not just on the Black Friday period. Making you a master when it comes to buying and always ensuring a better price on your products. Congratulations on getting here! After all the tips described in this reading, I can assure you that you will save more on your purchases. Always seek to practice the knowledge acquired here to be a happier and a more organized consumer in your life.

About.

Today as a technology professional, as a consumer and a user of services, like everyone else, I was able to express my knowledge here in this EBook.

I apologize to those more demanding that this is my first produced EBook. But I'm sure this reading could help many of you.

I will be launching with this EBook a store of mine with the company BlessTec. I will make more digital content available in the future including some apps that i´ve never released on the market.

If you, dear reader, have enjoyed this work and would even like to recommend it to someone else or comment on your opinion, please subscribe to the email below for future notifications. And don't forget to share this EBook with friends and family. The more we spread this financial education content the better the market will be for us consumers.

EBook Contact Email:

support@en.manualblackfridaymasters.com

Recommend this work:

https://www.manualblackfridaymasters.com/

Thank you very much,

Washington Luiz de Figueiredo Junior.

www.ingramcontent.com/pod-product-compliance
Lightning Source LLC
Chambersburg PA
CBHW040347220526
45473CB00009B/2805